Paint Me a Poem

Poems Inspired by Masterpieces of Art

JUSTINE ROWDEN

WORDSONG

BOYDS MILLS PRESS

SPECK
Sam Francis
National Gallery of Art, Washington
Gift of Gemini G.E.L.
(American, 1923–1994; date of lithograph, 1971)

ZIGGIDY, ZAGGEDY

Ziggidy, jiggidy colors
Jaggedy, zaggedy music;
Maraschino-cherry reds
Chevy Blazer blues
Mustard yellows
Lime jello greens.

Listen to them zaggedy at each other—
The reds, cymbals,
Greens, flutes,
Blues, cellos
Yellows, trumpets,
What wild sounds,
What fantastic music!

With My Father

Come and I will tell you
About when *I* was a little girl,
How I rode on horseback
Through the countryside
Holding onto my father
As we rode
Down quiet roads.

And when we would come to an inn,
We would stop,
And he would buy me
Cider and freshly baked bread.
He would tell me I was really a princess;
I would always be one.

And then we rode back to town,
The princess holding onto her father.

GREEN PLUMS
Joseph Decker

National Gallery of Art, Washington

Collection of Mr. and Mrs Paul Mellon

(American, 1853–1924; date of painting, c.1885)

Dancin'

Green plums rolling
Yeah! rockin' and rollin'
Out of their box
Onto the stage
Ready to swing their stems,
Moving in rhythm
To a juicy tune.
The beat, it gets to them—
Swaying side to side,
They go even faster

Until finger-snapping hands
Put them back in their box.

faster, *Faster,* ***FASTER !***

Why, of course, it's George
Riding toward Valley Forge.

faster, *Faster,* ***FASTER !***

Trotting into surrounded towns,

faster, *Faster,* ***FASTER !***

Racing onto snowy roads,

faster, *Faster,* ***FASTER !***

Galloping into friendly glens,

faster, *Faster,* ***FASTER !***

Why, it's George, of course,
Astride, indeed, his big white horse.

GENERAL WASHINGTON ON A WHITE CHARGER

Anonymous

National Gallery of Art, Washington

Gift of Edgar William and Bernice Chrysler Garbisch

(American, 19th century; date of painting, 1835 or after)

KEELMEN HEAVING IN COALS BY MOONLIGHT

Joseph Mallord William Turner

National Gallery of Art, Washington

Widener Collection

(British, 1775–1851; date of painting, 1835)

NOISY NIGHT AT SEA

NOISY BELLS CLANG
   FURLED SAILS JANGLE
      CRIES LOUD AND BRASH
         AS WOODEN HULLS RASP.

FIERCE COMMANDS CALL
   RED EMBERS FALL
      IN WATER DARK AND COLD;
         BARRELS ROCKING IN THE HOLD.

MORE SCREAMS, "WATCH OUT!"
   A SMALL BOAT COMES ABOUT.
      NOISES, SCREECHES, YELLS,
         FURTHER SCREAMING OF THE BELLS.

NO CALM IN THIS PORT
   WHILE FIRES CAVORT
      HURLING FRENZIED LIGHT
         INTO THE WATERY NIGHT.

MEADOW
Alfred Sisley
National Gallery of Art, Washington
Ailsa Mellon Bruce Collection
(French, 1839–1899; date of painting, 1875)

Moving White Fluffs

The sky is full
Of fuzzy white polka dots.
As they move on,
Do you think
Those white dots are really
Dancing the polka
While they drift away?

Doing the polka
Takes time to learn
And where could they
Hear the music
To get the dance just right?
So, maybe it's not
The polka at all they're doing.

Maybe it's just a slow glide
They make up
As they go along.
Then why do you suppose
They call them "Polka dots"—
Those fuzzy white fluffs
In the blue, blue sky?

W H O O S H !

The rosy red that starts
At the bottom
Is like a softened breeze,
A gentle wind that brushes
Against the cheeks of a daffodil
And makes the petals laugh.

The red in the middle
Is a bustling wind
That makes branches
Reach out in huge leaps
To tag the next tree
And quickly whip back and hide.

At the very top;
The rich dark red
Is a wild, furious gust
That makes kites somersault,
And pull even higher
To catch a passing plane

And race it through to a cloud.

UNTITLED
Mark Rothko

National Gallery of Art, Washington
Gift of the Mark Rothko Foundation
(American, 1903–1970; date of painting, 1967)

Oh So Perfect

The ladies with hats that flatter

Don't permit cups to clatter

Nor tea to splatter

On silvery platters.

And humorous chatter

Leaves them so much gladder,

And that's what matters

    To the ladies

    With hats

    That flatter.

THE VISIT
Édouard Vuillard
National Gallery of Art, Washington
Chester Dale Collection
(French, 1868–1940; date of painting, 1931)

FLOWERS IN A VASE

André Derain

National Gallery of Art, Washington

Chester Dale Collection

(French, 1880–1954; date of painting, 1932)

SO CLOSE

You seem to be awfully close;
Your stem is stepping on my toes.

I don't think so.

Could you please tuck your leaves in a little bit?

There's really no place to move.

At least, could you please try not to lean on me?

I don't think I really am.
Your petals are in my face; they're blocking my view.

That's just the way I happen to blossom.

Could we try to get along?
You know, you are an incredible shade of pink.

Oh, you noticed!   *I'm really glad you're so close.*

It's All Hidden

Sometimes a surprise
    is meant to be hidden,
        where no one suspects
            what secrets are there—

Like a delicate green bud
    quietly sleeping,
        waiting for morning
            to burst into purple.

Or a marshmallow-white egg
    hiding a golden yolk
        deep, deep inside
            its serene white oval.

And that black silk hat
    sitting tall on a head,
        laughing, for it knows
            it is really red inside.

BARTOLOMÉ SUREDA Y MISEROL
Francisco de Goya
National Gallery of Art, Washington
Gift of Mr. and Mrs. P. H. B. Frelinghuysen in memory
of her father and mother, Mr. and Mrs. H. O. Havemeyer
(Spanish, 1746–1828; date of painting, c.1803–1804)

MOUNTAINS AT COLLIOURE
André Derain

National Gallery of Art, Washington

John Hay Whitney Collection

(French, 1880–1954; date of painting, 1905)

Purple in My Path

The mountains are the orange of melons
The valleys are blue, a velvety blue.
The sky's green, a silk of green,
And the path, the path's all lavender–purple.

I know who made this happen!
It's that round magician
High in the sky
Laughing in her veil of gold.

But in an hour it will all have faded,
All will be quiet and dark . . .
No longer the melon and lavender
That seem so enchanted.

GINEVRA de' BENCI

Leonardo da Vinci

National Gallery of Art, Washington

Ailsa Mellon Bruce Fund

(Italian, 1452–1519; date of painting, c.1474)

TWIRLING

Curls twirling

Like water

Whirling,

Swirling;

Chasing

Racing

Curlicues.

WOMAN WITH AMPHORA AND POMEGRANATES
Henri Matisse
National Gallery of Art, Washington
Ailsa Mellon Bruce Fund
(French, 1869–1954; date of painting, 1953)

BLUE

It's a wonderful blue:

Not the blue of a cool lake, where rowboats glide
    into waves that greet them,
        splashing against the sides like high-fives,

Not the blue of a ripe blueberry about to join its cousins
    in a plump blueberry pie,
        with all the berries snuggling up against each other,

Not the blue of the sky on a hot,
    windless summer day,
        when even the trees and the grass are caught napping.

Its own blue,
A wonderful blue,

BLUE.

Don't I Know You?

Say, you standing out there
    Looking at my little ones
        Playing with the ball of red yarn,
        You look familiar;
            I think I know YOU!

Weren't you the one who asked
    If mother cats
        Ever wore sunglasses?

Then didn't you ask
    If I ever got a babysitter
        For my tiny babies?

And weren't you the one
    Who complained that
        My children
            Were behaving
                As badly
                    As little kittens!

Well, it was certainly someone who looked like you!

CAT AND KITTENS

Anonymous

National Gallery of Art, Washington

Gift of Edgar William and Bernice Chrysler Garbisch

(American, 19th century; date of painting, c.1872–1883)

NOTES ABOUT THE ARTISTS

SAM FRANCIS
Speck

Sam Francis's paintings are full of playful color. His art is called abstract because it doesn't represent lifelike objects or scenes. The colors and shapes in his paintings dance and move. The artist seems to have been running and rushing with joy when he painted. He tickles us by using layers of colors. See if you can find where he has done that in *Speck*.

AUGUSTE RENOIR
Madame Henriot

We see the love of beauty in Renoir's paintings. Renoir said that he wanted his paintings to be lovely scenes. His colors are wonderful—as luscious as ice cream. The light is brilliant, and there is a sense of happiness in his paintings.

JOSEPH DECKER
Green Plums

Decker came to the United States when he was fourteen years old. He first worked as a house painter and sign painter. After taking drawing classes, he found he loved to paint simple and familiar objects. His paintings of fruit call to us because they are so luscious.

ANONYMOUS
General Washington on a White Charger

This portrait was done when the United States was just beginning. Traveling artists, sometimes called journeymen painters, went from town to town offering to paint the portraits of a family.

In this case, a family must have wanted a painting that would occupy a prominent place in their home—a painting of a famous person. So they requested a painting of the most famous person in the country at the time—George Washington.

These traveling painters often did not sign their work, so we say these artists are anonymous.

JOSEPH MALLORD WILLIAM TURNER
Keelmen Heaving in Coals by Moonlight

Turner first exhibited his art when he was only thirteen years old. He displayed his drawings in the front window of his father's shop.

Turner's paintings are like sets for a play; they are dramatic in color and light and atmosphere. Turner makes us feel as though we are right onstage in the play.

ALFRED SISLEY
Meadow

Sisley wanted his paintings to sing with gentle colors. He loved creating landscapes that are soft, gentle, lovely. A faint hum seems to fill his pictures.

And one element that is extremely important in each painting is—the SKY.

MARK ROTHKO
Untitled

Rothko's paintings are unusual designs, rather than objects or scenes we recognize. We call this art abstract. What strong colors! What powerful reds! Rothko left his paintings untitled. By doing this, he asks us to search our own imagination to find a story that fits with each painting.

ÉDOUARD VUILLARD
The Visit

Vuillard loved to do paintings of rooms in Paris that he knew. The rooms he depicts have so many interesting details, but Vuillard wanted to hint at the stories that went on in these rooms, too. He liked to say that he didn't want to tell all the stories, all the secrets. So he left it to us to fill in those stories.

ANDRÉ DERAIN
Flowers in a Vase
Mountains at Collioure

Derain loved to use wild, fanciful colors. He belonged to a group in Paris who loved to paint in this same imaginative way. Some people called these artists wild, wild animals. "Fauve!" they would shout in French. Even today, we call Derain and his fellow artists who painted with abandon "Fauvists" or "Fauve." But now, to be in that group is a mark of honor.

FRANCISCO de GOYA
Bartolomé Sureda y Miserol

As an artist, Goya was always experimenting. At a time when painters created portraits of men with their hats firmly on their heads, Goya showed us a different way to present an elegant man—holding his hat. The man is not stiff—but quite calm—perhaps about to tell us he'd like us to join him for a fancy dessert.

LEONARDO da VINCI
Ginevra de' Benci

Leonardo doesn't let us know exactly what Ginevra is thinking. We wonder, and we each come up with a different story—which is probably exactly what Leonardo meant us to do.

Leonardo proposed scientific puzzles to himself, after which he would work on the solution. One of those puzzles was to figure out a way to make special glasses to see the moon enlarged.

HENRI MATISSE
Woman with Amphora and Pomegranates

After painting for most of his life, Matisse was too ill as an older man to stand at the easel and paint. So he used his talents to make wonderful cutouts with paper and scissors—just the materials children use. He carefully arranged the cutouts to make striking collages. Matisse thought these collages were like sculptures. And he especially loved using the color blue.

ANONYMOUS
Cat and Kittens

Those early journeymen painters who traveled to towns hoped to find work painting family portraits or, perhaps, family pets. These painters were self-taught. The paintings are often exaggerated in some way and not exactly true to life—but that only makes them seem more lovable to us now.

FOR MARC

My gratitude
to Barbara Moore
of the National Gallery of Art for her
generous encouragement and assistance;
to Jean Spring
for the waves of enthusiasm that buoyed my spirits;
and
to my patient and ever-constructive editor,
Wendy Murray.

—J. R.

Text copyright © 2005 by Justine Rowden
Images © Board of Trustees, National Gallery of Art, Washington
All rights reserved.
Published by Wordsong
Boyds Mills Press, Inc., A Highlights Company
815 Church Street, Honesdale, Pennsylvania 18431
Printed in China
Visit our Web site at www.boydsmillspress.com

Publisher Cataloging-in-Publication Data (U.S.)
Rowden, Justine.
Paint me a poem : poems inspired by masterpieces of art
Summary: Poems written in response to fourteen paintings from
the National Gallery of Art, Washington
paired with color reproductions of the artwork.
ISBN 1-59078-289-5
1. Poetry. 2. Fine Art—Poetry. I. Rowden, Justine. II. Title.
811.54

First edition, 2005
10 9 8 7 6 5 4 3 2 1
Book designed by Mina Greenstein

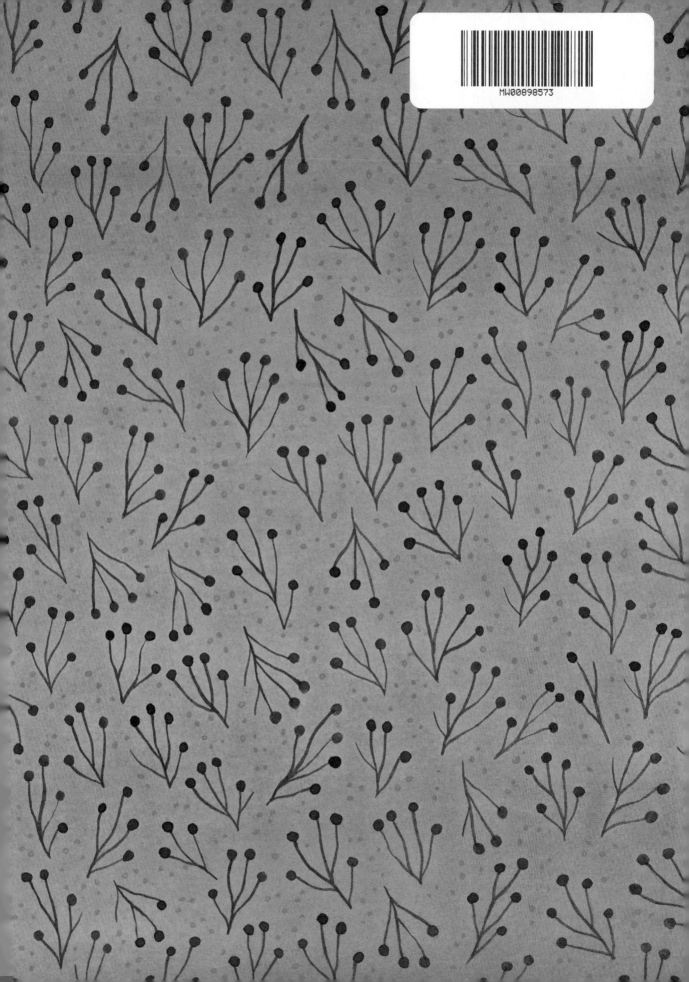

A mi familia panda.
A ti por multiplicarte conmigo. Ya no somos dos, somos cuatro.
A vosotras, nuestras dos oseznas. La osa mayor y la osa menor entre las constelaciones.
Vuestros abrazos de oso son el universo entero. Cuando se pare
el tiempo para mí, que sea en un abrazo infinito.

Asko maite zaituztet. Hemendik izaterretaraino eta buelta.

Papel certificado por el Forest Stewardship Council®

MIXTO
Papel procedente de
fuentes responsables
FSC® C117695

Primera edición: marzo de 2020

Printed in Spain – Impreso en España

ISBN: 978-84-488-5436-2
Depósito legal: B-437-2020

Diseño y maquetación: LimboStudio

Impreso en Soler Talleres Gráficos
Esplugues de Llobregat (Barcelona)

BE 5 4 3 6 A

Penguin
Random House
Grupo Editorial

No sé qué pasa hoy en casa...

Todos están muy contentos.
Más contentos de lo normal.

Poco a poco, la barriga de Mamá Panda irá creciendo y creciendo hasta que se haga tan grande como una sandía. Después... ¡saldrá el bebé! Y seremos uno más en la familia.

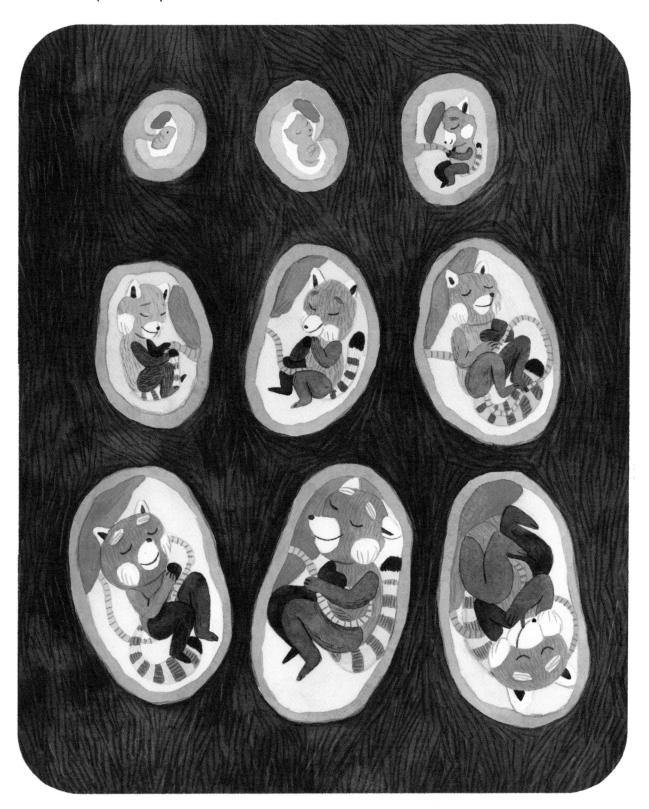

Pues sí que ha crecido ese bebé...
Debe de ser enorme porque ahora mamá parece
más una ballena que una osa panda roja.

Come más que el abuelo,

pero todo le sienta mal.

Cuando corro, ya no me pilla.

Le vendría bien un pañal.

Y siempre siempre tiene sueño.

Hasta se le ha olvidado cómo
se hacen las cosas más sencillas.

Papá dice que mi hermanita está a gusto nadando
en la barriga de mamá y que no quiere salir.

¡Claro! Mamá tendrá una superpiscina ahí dentro.
Cuando salga le dejaré la mía.

A veces le canto canciones y le doy besos.
Ella me saluda con pataditas.

Todavía no sabe que se saluda con la mano.

Hoy por la mañana, cuando me he despertado,
no estaba mamá, ni papá...
Estaban los abuelos y ha sido como un día de fiesta.

Por la tarde hemos ido al hospital en el coche del abuelo.

Li huele a caramelo, y es suave como mi peluche.

Mamá lleva un pijama raro y papá ha dormido en una silla.
Tienen ojeras como los otros osos panda, los blancos y negros.

Por fin estamos todos en casa.

Ya no somos tres.

Ahora somos uno más.

¡Papáááá!
¿Y el final del
cuento?

Al principio no me gustaba nada ser uno más.

Mamá ya no es solo mi mamá.

Y papá tampoco.

Ni la abuela, ni el abuelo.

Ni la otra abuela, ni el otro abuelo, ni la tía, ni mi primo...

Pero un día hice un truco de magia, y mi
hermana se rio a carcajadas y no podía parar.
¡Casi se mea de la risa!

Hasta se ha aprendido mi nombre.

Es como tener una mascota.

Mejor aún...

Como una amiga...

Más que una amiga...

¡SALTAAAA!

¡Es mi hermana! ¡Mi hermana pequeña!

¡HASTA LA LUNA!

La familia Conejo nos ha invitado a una fiesta de cumpleaños.

¡Hoy será un gran día!

FIN.

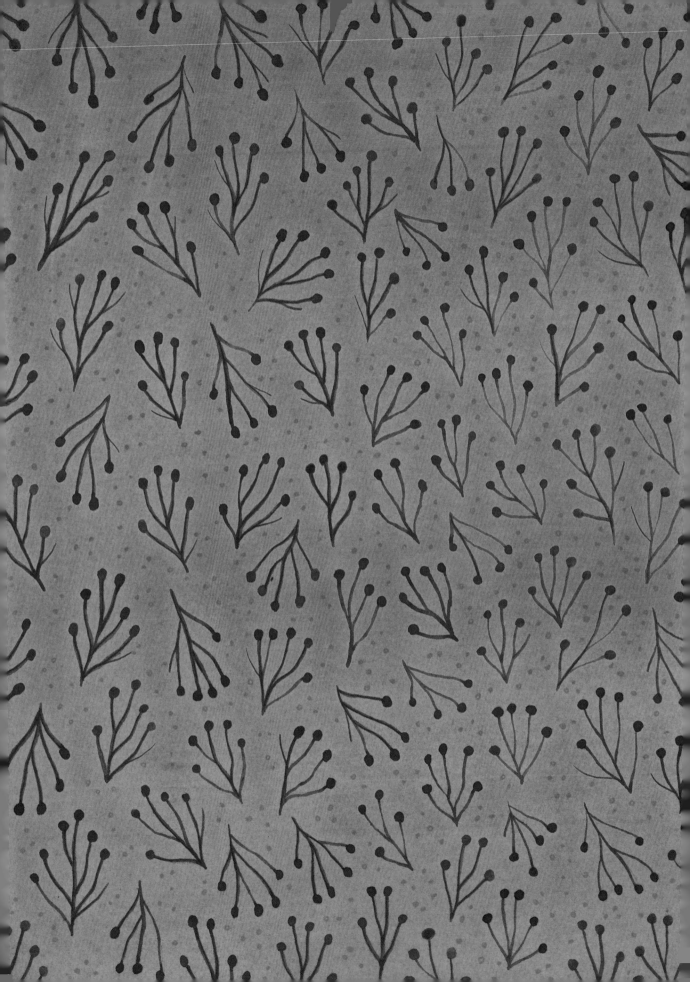